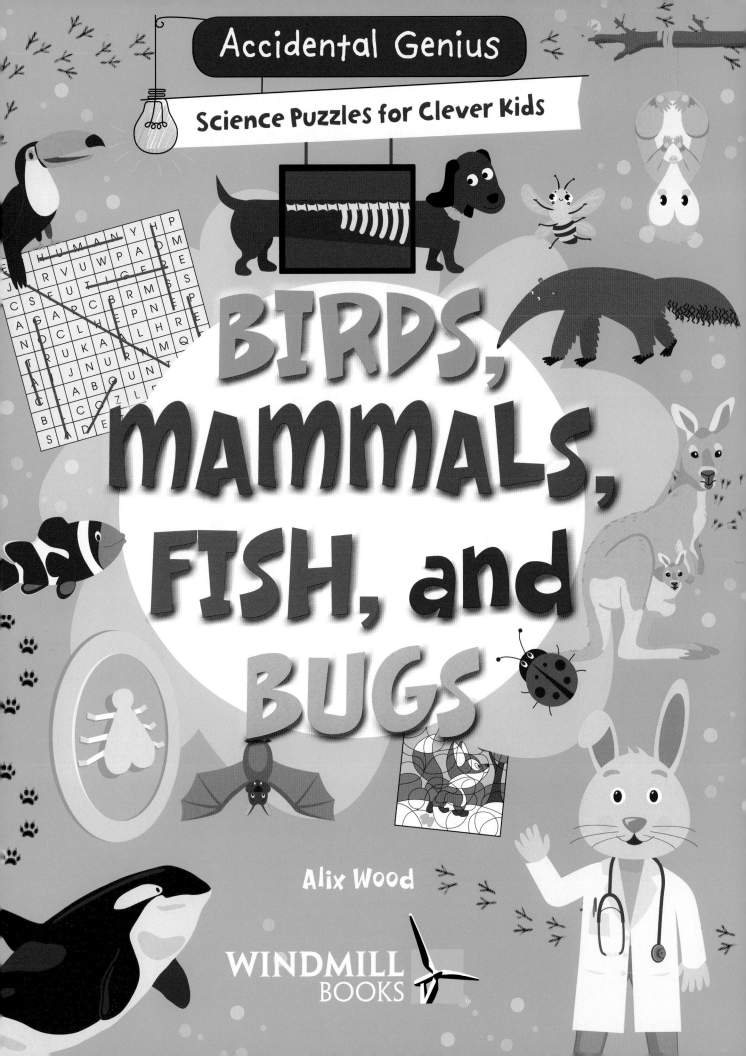

Accidental Genius

Science Puzzles for Clever Kids

BIRDS, MAMMALS, FISH, and BUGS

Alix Wood

WINDMILL BOOKS

Photocopy, print, or trace the puzzles if you are sharing this book with others. Then you won't spoil the book for the next person.

Published in 2023 by Windmill Books,
an Imprint of Rosen Publishing
29 East 21st Street, New York, NY 10010

Copyright © 2021 Alix Wood Books

Written and designed by Alix Wood

Printed in the United States of America

CPSIA Compliance Information: Batch CSWM23: For Further Information contact Rosen Publishing, New York, New York at 1-800-237-9932

Cataloging-in-Publication Data

Names: Wood, Alix.
Title: Birds, mammals, fish, and bugs / Alix Wood.
Description: New York : Windmill Publishing, 2023. | Series: Accidental genius: science puzzles for clever kids
Identifiers: ISBN 9781508198529 (pbk.) | ISBN 9781508198536 (library bound) | ISBN 9781508198543 (ebook)
Subjects: LCSH: Puzzles--Juvenile literature. | Picture puzzles--Juvenile literature. | Games--Juvenile literature. | Animals--Juvenile literature.
Classification: LCC GV1493.W66 2023 | DDC 793.73--dc23

Find us on

Contents

So Many Animals

The world is full of millions of animals. There are furry ones and feathery ones, cute ones and scary ones. They are all so different! So what do all these creatures have in common?

Animals are living things.

Animals eat other living things, such as plants, or other animals.

Animals have senses, such as sight, hearing, touch, or smell. Their senses help them find food, mates, and safety.

Plants are alive, but they are not animals. What's the difference between a plant and an animal? Plants make their own food. Animals can't do this. Animals eat plants or other animals.

Because there are SO many animals, scientists come up with ways to sort them into groups. First, they sort them into whether or not they have a backbone.

Animals that have a backbone are called vertebrates.

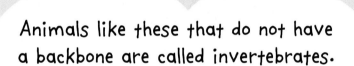

Animals like these that do not have a backbone are called invertebrates.

Animal Groups

Hundreds of animals have backbones, and thousands of animals don't have backbones! Scientists use other special words to sort them all into smaller groups. I bet you know some of the words already. Try this quick test.

What would you call these creatures?

They live underwater.
They breathe through their gills.
They have fins to help them swim.
They have scales on their bodies.

fins

scales

gills

Word Jumble

These circles of letters are jumbled-up words. Unscramble the letters to see if you were right.

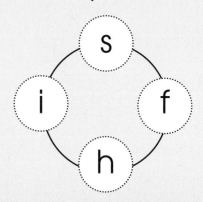

s
i
f
h

What would you call these?

wings

feathers

beak

claws

r
b
d
s
i

What about these creatures?

Most have wings.

Most have antennae.

Word Jumble

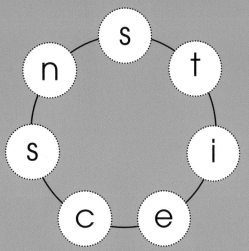

n
s
t
s
i
c
e

They have 6 legs.

They don't have a backbone. They have a hard outer shell instead.

Mammals Make Milk

What do you, your dog, and a giraffe all have in common? You are all mammals. Mammals are animals whose babies drink their mother's milk. Mammals come in all shapes and sizes.

All mammals have hair.

All mammals make milk to feed their young.

Mammals are warm-blooded. That means their body is the same temperature, no matter how cold or hot the place they live gets.

Awkward Mammals!

Mammals babies are born live, not from eggs.

Except echidnas!

All mammals have teeth.

Except anteaters!

Mammals can't fly.

Except bats!

Mammal Word Search

Can you find the ten mammals hiding in this grid?

ELEPHANT
DOG
HORSE
BEAR
HUMAN
WHALE
TIGER
CAT
SHEEP
GORILLA

E	T	H	U	M	A	N	Y	H	P
J	L	R	V	U	W	A	A	O	M
C	S	E	U	T	I	G	E	R	E
A	G	A	P	C	B	R	M	S	S
N	O	C	H	H	E	P	N	E	P
T	R	A	K	A	A	L	H	R	E
A	I	R	N	U	R	N	M	Q	E
C	L	A	B	G	U	N	T	L	H
B	L	C	O	C	L	E	G	R	S
S	A	D	E	T	W	H	A	L	E

Did you know dolphins and whales feed their young milk? That makes them mammals, too. They even have hair! Dolphins have a few whiskers when they are born. Whales have hair, too, but you can hardly see it.

9

How Many Legs?

Some animals have two legs. Some have six, and others have hundreds. There are some animals that have no legs at all!

Can you match each animal in the pictures to the sentences below?

Birds have two legs.

Insects have six legs.

Spiders have eight legs.

Snakes don't have any legs.

Millipedes have so many legs it's hard to count!

These are NOT legs! Many insects have antennae they use to touch and smell things. Spiders have palps which they use like arms.

antennae 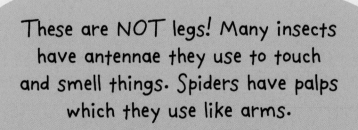 palps

Insect Hunt

Can you find ten insects hiding in this picture? Remember, insects have six legs, not eight, so beware of the spiders!

Walking on the Ceiling!

Have you watched a fly walk upside down? How do they do that? Flies have really clever feet. Their feet ooze a special wet glue made of sugars and oil. The glue is just strong enough so the fly can walk up walls and across ceilings!

How Does It Work?

You will need: a pencil, some thin printer paper, scissors, a saucer, some water

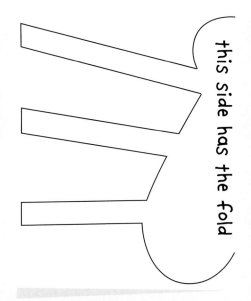

this side has the fold

1. Fold the paper in half. Draw this shape on the paper and then cut it out.

2. Open up the paper. Bend the legs down. Then bend the feet over.

3. Wet the feet with water. Hold a saucer upright. Place your fly's damp feet on the saucer, and then let go. Your fly should stick!

Spiders spin webs to catch other bugs to eat. They lie with their legs spread out on the web and wait. Tiny hairs on their legs wobble if the web moves. Then they know they have caught a snack!

Join the Dots

What is walking toward this spider's web? Why do you think it might escape?

7
8
6
9
5 11 10
4 12
2 3 13
1 14
15

Spiders tiptoe around their webs so they don't get caught!

Reptiles

What do lizards, snakes, turtles, crocodiles, and alligators have in common? They are all reptiles. Reptiles are cold-blooded. Their body temperature changes when the temperature around them changes. Most reptiles sleep during the cold months. This is called hibernation.

Reptiles have a backbone. Most reptiles have four legs. Snakes have none.

Reptiles' bodies are covered in scales.

Most reptiles lay eggs. Can you find three eggs in this picture?

Reptiles may live in water, on land, under the ground, or in trees.

These giant reptiles used to roam Earth. Copy the grid below, then copy the drawing in each square into the correct square on your grid. What did you draw?

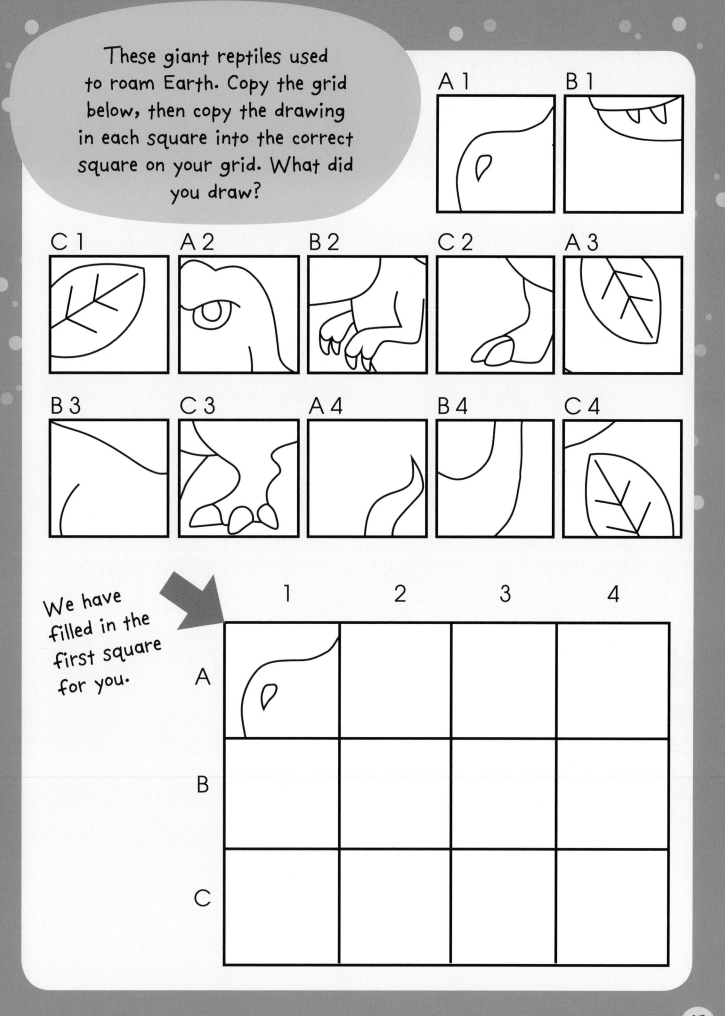

A 1   B 1

C 1   A 2   B 2   C 2   A 3

B 3   C 3   A 4   B 4   C 4

We have filled in the first square for you.

1   2   3   4

A

B

C

Animals with Pockets!

Marsupials are mammals that usually carry their young in a special pouch. Their young are very tiny when they are born. To survive, they need to cling to their mother and drink her milk. Kangaroos, koalas, and opossums are all marsupials.

Kangaroos live in Australia. There are lots of marsupials in Australia and New Guinea.

Asia

New Guinea

Australia

A baby kangaroo is called a joey.

Once their babies are big enough, they can leave the pouch. Marsupial babies still run to the pouch or cling to their mother's fur if there is any danger.

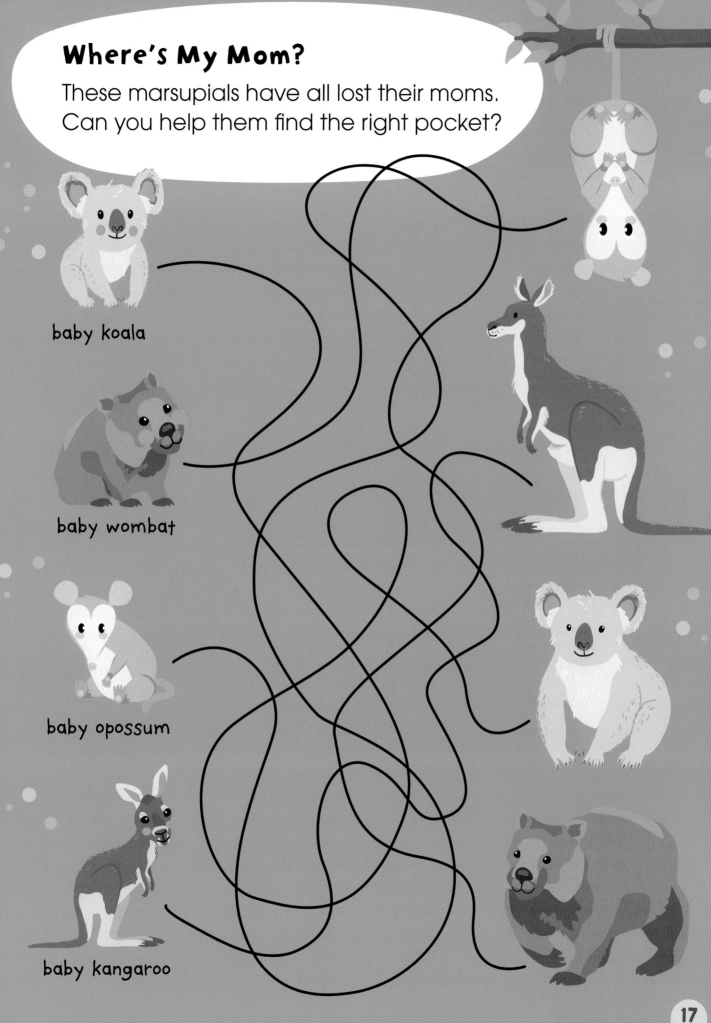

Where's My Mom?

These marsupials have all lost their moms. Can you help them find the right pocket?

baby koala

baby wombat

baby opossum

baby kangaroo

Hunter or Hunted?

Animals that hunt other animals are called predators. The animals they hunt are called prey. One way to tell if an animal is prey or predator is to look at their eyes.

Prey have eyes on the sides of their head. Side-facing eyes help them spot animals creeping up on them.

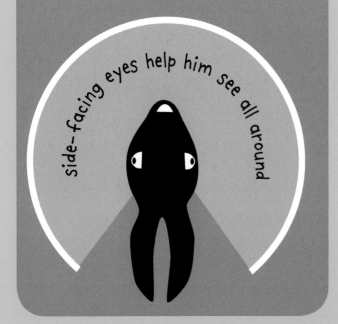

side-facing eyes help him see all around

Predators have eyes on the front of their head. Forward-facing eyes help the hunter tell how far away prey is, and how fast it is moving.

forward-facing eyes help her hunt

Most apes don't hunt, they eat plants. Why do they have forward-facing eyes? To help them see how far a branch is as they swing through the trees!

Prey or Predator?

Find the predator in these pairs of prey and predator.

Remember to look at their eyes

A predator is not always bigger than its prey.

Perfect Feet

Animals use their feet to dig, climb, swim, run, and eat. An animal's feet can tell you a lot about its life. They have just the right feet to do the things they need to do. Look at these animals' feet from underneath.

Bears have strong claws to help them dig and rip insects out of tree bark.

Ducks have webbed feet to help push themselves through water.

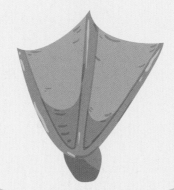

Camels have wide, flat feet to keep them from sinking in the sand.

Tree frogs have grippy, webbed feet. Their feet ooze fluid to keep them clean!

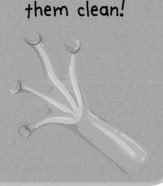

Goats have two toes. That helps them balance as they climb.

Horses' hooves protect their feet on hard ground.

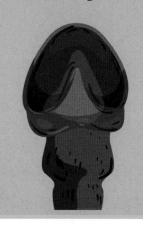

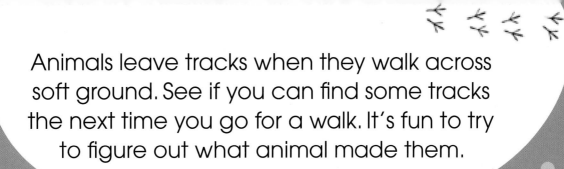

Animals leave tracks when they walk across soft ground. See if you can find some tracks the next time you go for a walk. It's fun to try to figure out what animal made them.

Try Tracking

Which animals make these footprints?
Follow the tracks to find out.

A

B

C

bear

goat

horse

Surviving the Heat

Deserts can be hot, dry, sandy places. They also can be hard places to live. But some birds, reptiles, mammals, and insects happily make the desert their home. They have clever ways to survive the heat and the lack of water.

Camels store fat in their humps. They use the stored fat for food on long desert journeys.

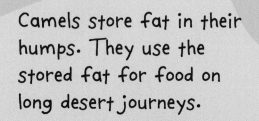

Ostriches can go a long time without drinking. They get water from the plants they eat.

Porcupines hide underground or in the shade in the daytime.

Shadow Match

Can you match each shadow to the correct desert animal?

porcupine	rattlesnake	ostrich
camel	bobcat	vulture

A vulture urinates on its legs to cool itself down!

In summer, a bobcat's gray fur changes to a sandy color. This makes it easy to hide when it hunts.

A rattlesnake can hunt in complete darkness. A special pit on its head senses heat coming from its prey!

Who Is in the Trees?

Trees give shelter and food. A mouse may hide in a hole in the trunk when it rains. Sloths sleep in the branches. Birds build nests in them. Monkeys eat their fruit. Lemurs snack on the flowers and bark. Chameleons eat insects hiding in the leaves. Snakes climb trees too, to hunt from above.

Can you find the tree frog?

Odd One Out

Which animal does not spend time in trees?

A

B

C

D

Do a Big Tree Animal Count

Scientists record what animals live in different places. Do your own animal count!

You will need: a large pale sheet, a pen and paper, a camera, a tray, and some damp soil

1. Find a big tree. Take an adult with you. Sit quietly and watch your tree for an hour. Count any birds and animals that come. Photograph them if you can.

2. Lay the sheet under a branch. Gently shake the branch. You don't want to damage the tree or hurt the bugs. Quickly photograph what fell onto the sheet. You can find out what they all are later. Let the bugs go.

3. Put some damp soil on a flat tray. Leave it at the base of the tree overnight. Did you get any little footprints? Look them up to see what animals came to your tree.

Living in the Cold

Some animals are designed for cold weather. Polar bears are covered with warm, thick fur. They even have fur on the bottoms of their feet! This helps them grip on the slippery ice. Polar bears and seals have a layer of fat called blubber. Blubber helps keep them warm in cold water.

How Does Blubber Keep You Warm?

You will need: three ziplock freezer bags, a block of shortening, duct tape, bowl, cold water, ice cubes

1. Fill two ziplock bags with a thick layer of shortening. Seal the bags shut.
2. Duct tape the two bags together on three sides to make a fat blubber mitten.
3. Put some cold water and the ice cubes in a bowl.
4. Put one hand in the remaining ziplock bag, and the other hand in the blubber mitten. You could ask someone to tape the mittens to your wrists.
5. Put both hands in the icy water.

Which hand feels the coldest? Can you keep the blubber mitten hand in the water for longer?

Arctic foxes are gray in summer. They grow a thick coat of white fur in winter. This keeps them warm and helps them hide in the snow. It is easier to hunt when your prey can't see you.

an arctic fox in summer

Can You Find the Fox?

Photocopy and color the picture to find the hidden arctic fox.

Use these colors

| 1 | 2 | 3 | 4 | 5 |

Now it's Summertime!

Living Underground

Some animals head underground to keep cool in summer, or warm in winter. Life can be safer underground, too. Rabbits dig burrows to sleep in. Moles and earthworms spend their whole lives underground. Coyotes dig dens to raise their young.

Next time you see a hole in the soil, look for tracks nearby. You might be able to find out who lives there!

Underground Animals Word Search

Find ten animals that spend time underground.

MOLE
RABBIT
BADGER
EARTHWORM
TOAD
GROUNDHOG
VOLE
FOX
DORMOUSE
ANT

E	T	H	G	M	A	N	D	H	P
J	E	A	R	T	H	W	O	R	M
C	S	E	O	T	I	R	R	R	F
A	G	A	U	C	E	R	M	S	J
N	O	C	N	G	E	P	O	T	X
T	O	A	D	A	A	L	U	I	E
A	I	A	H	M	V	N	S	B	E
C	B	R	O	G	O	N	E	B	H
B	L	C	G	L	L	L	G	A	S
S	F	O	X	T	E	H	E	R	E

In the Water

More than 70 percent of our planet is covered by water! So many animals live in lakes, rivers, ponds, and the ocean. Fish spend all their time underwater. Crocodiles, crabs, frogs, and turtles spend some time on land too. Mammals living in water come to the surface to breathe.

Amphibians

Amphibians are born in water. The young breathe through gills like a fish. Then they grow lungs to breathe air. Now they can live on land. Frogs and newts are amphibians.

baby frogs are called tadpoles

Can you find
the seahorse?

A whale is a mammal.
It comes to the surface for air.

Seagulls float on the
water looking for fish.

Sea turtles cannot breathe
underwater, but they can hold
their breath for a long time.

Jellyfish don't have
a brain or eyes!

Octopuses like to
hide in the seaweed.

Crabs walk along
the ocean floor.

Animal Houses

Some animals are amazing builders! They make perfect houses from the natural things they find where they live. You can help wildlife find safe places to live, too. Put up a nest box. Or leave out some soft straw or animal hair for them to use to line their nests.

Birds build nests to bring up their young.

Nesting boxes make a safe home for birds.

Squirrels build nests called dreys.

Beavers build homes called lodges from sticks and mud.

Can You Build a Nest?

You will need: twigs, moss, feathers, leaves, grass, and mud

1. Have a close-up look at some bird nests. See if you can tell how the bird made them. Wash your hands well afterward if you touch the nest.
2. Try to make a nest out of the materials you've gathered. It's not as easy as it looks! You may want to try weaving grass and twigs around into a circle.
3. You can add some sticky mud to glue your twigs and grass in place.
4. Line your nest with moss, leaves, and feathers.

Would your nest survive in the wind or rain?
Could it hold an egg safely?

Turtles can hide in their own shell if there is danger.

Bees live together in a hive.

Foxes build a den underground.

Hedgehogs may make their nests among tree roots.

Meat or Plants?

Different animals eat different types of food. Giraffes only eat plants. Tigers only eat meat. Bears eat meat and plants.

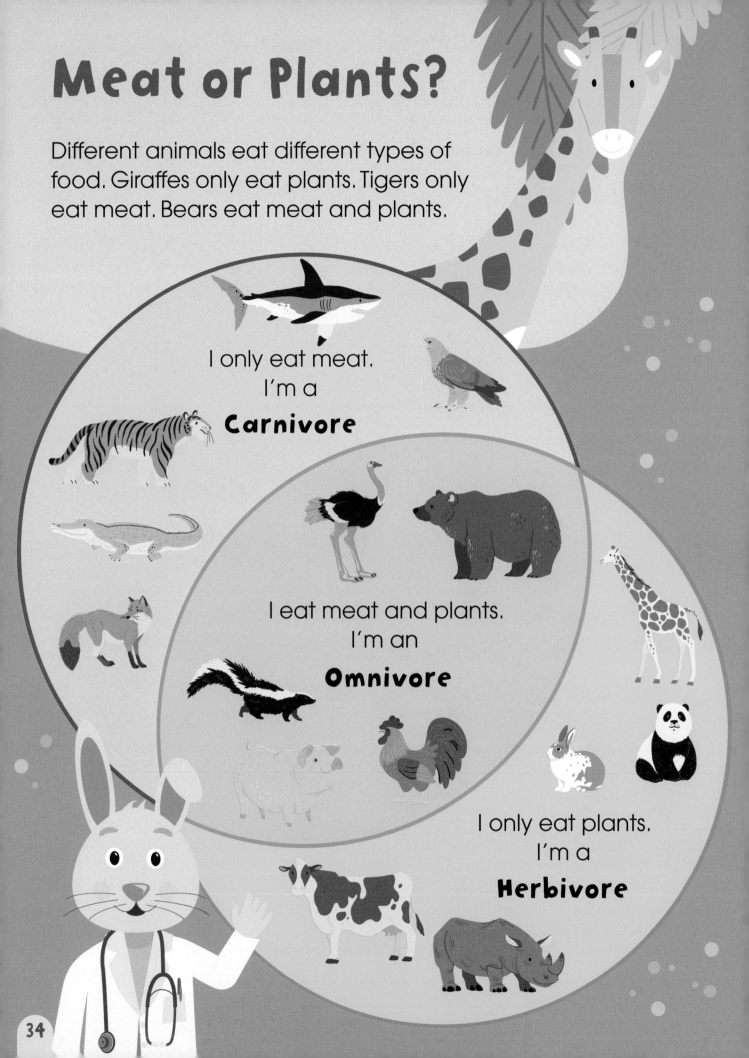

I only eat meat.
I'm a
Carnivore

I eat meat and plants.
I'm an
Omnivore

I only eat plants.
I'm a
Herbivore

Omnivore, Herbivore, Carnivore?

Do these animals eat meat, plants, or both?
Can you match them to the right bowl of food?

Quiz Time!

1. I only eat plants. What am I?

    a) a carnivore   b) a herbivore   c) an omnivore

2. True or false? Sharks are omnivores.

    a) true   b) false

Food Chains

All living things get energy from their food. Plants get energy from sunlight, water, and soil. Animals get energy from plants or other animals. A food chain is a line of living things that eat one another. All food chains start with the sun.

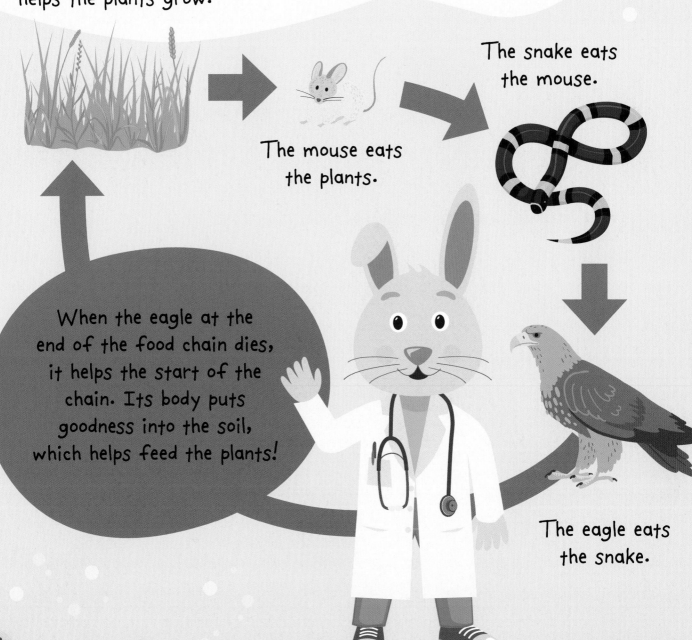

The sun's energy helps the plants grow.

The mouse eats the plants.

The snake eats the mouse.

The eagle eats the snake.

When the eagle at the end of the food chain dies, it helps the start of the chain. Its body puts goodness into the soil, which helps feed the plants!

Put these food chains in the right order.
1 is the food for 2, and 2 is the food for 3.
Use your finger to trace a line from each
animal to the right number in the chain.

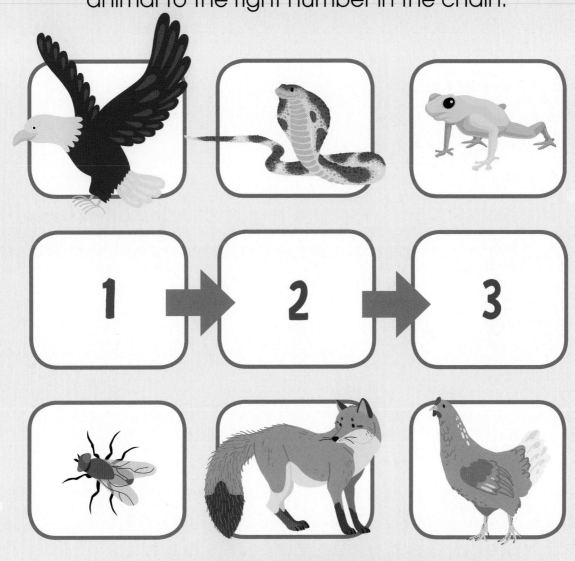

What 1, 2, 3 order do you think
this ocean food chain has?

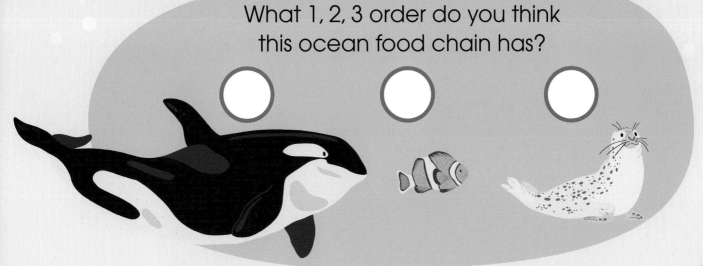

All About Eggs

What do birds, frogs, sea turtles, snails, and snakes all have in common? They all lay eggs! The eggs protect and feed the tiny animals as they grow. When they are ready, the babies hatch.

A bird's egg

The yellow yolk feeds the growing chick.

The egg white protects the chick and keeps it warm.

The shell has tiny holes which let air in and out.

Frogs lay their jellylike eggs in water. When they hatch, instead of a tiny frog, out swims a tiny tadpole! The tadpole gradually grows legs, loses its tail, and turns into a frog!

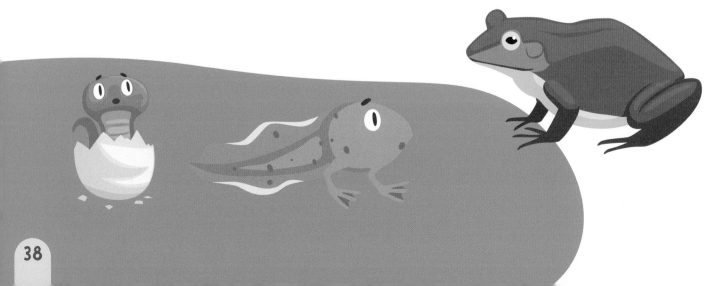

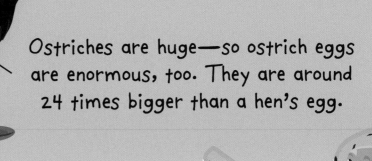

Ostriches are huge—so ostrich eggs are enormous, too. They are around 24 times bigger than a hen's egg.

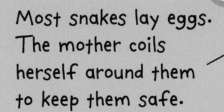

Most snakes lay eggs. The mother coils herself around them to keep them safe.

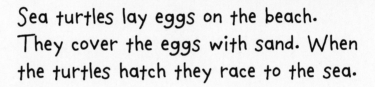

Sea turtles lay eggs on the beach. They cover the eggs with sand. When the turtles hatch they race to the sea.

Join the Dots

What is hatching out of this egg?

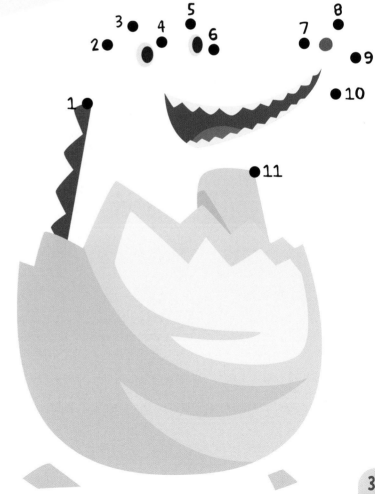

Animal Babies

The young of some animals have special names. A young dog is called a puppy. A baby cat is called a kitten. Do you know the names of these baby animals? Unscramble the letters to find out.

1

A young sheep is called a
M A L B
_ _ _ _ _

2

A young pig is called a
G I L P T E
_ _ _ _ _ _

3

A young cow is called a
A F L C
_ _ _ _

4

A young donkey is called a
O F L A
_ _ _ _

5

A young goat is called a
I D K
_ _ _

6

A young chicken is called a
H C K I C
_ _ _ _ _

Find the Parents

Did you know animal moms and dads have special names, too? Can you match the babies on page 40 with the right parents?

A hen   rooster

B jack   jenny

C nanny   billy

D cow   bull

E boar   sow

F ewe   ram

Night Animals

Most animals are active during the day, but some prefer to come out at night. When an animal is active at night, it is called nocturnal. Animals may sleep in the day because it is too hot. Or maybe they come out at night because what they hunt comes out at night! How do you think they find their way around in the dark?

great hearing

big eyes

Nocturnal animals often have big eyes that let in more light. Animals with poor eyesight find their way around using their other senses. Bats and owls have incredible hearing. Moths have a great sense of smell.

Spot the Day and Night Swaps

Can you find eight animal swaps in these two pictures?

Day

Night

43

Animal Genius Test

Are you an animal genius? Answer these animal questions to find out.

1 What do you call an animal that is active at night?

a) a carnivore

b) nocturnal

c) a mammal

2 How many legs does an insect have?

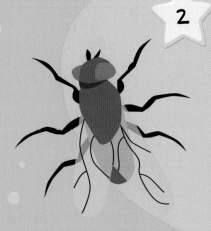

a) six

b) eight

c) two

3 Predators have eyes on the sides of their head. True or false?

4 Which of these animals doesn't lay eggs?

a) elephants

b) crocodiles

c) ostriches

5 What is the difference between a plant and an animal?

a) Animals have fur.

b) Plants are green.

c) Plants make their own food.

Answers

Page 6-7: the three word jumbles are: fish, birds, and insects.

Page 9:

E	T	H	U	M	A	N	Y	H	P
J	L	R	V	U	W	P	A	O	M
C	S	E	U	T	I	G	E	R	E
A	G	A	P	C	B	R	M	S	S
N	O	C	L	H	E	P	N	E	P
T	R	U	K	A	A	L	H	R	E
A	I	J	N	U	R	N	M	Q	E
C	L	A	B	G	U	N	T	L	H
B	L	C	O	Z	L	E	G	R	S
S	A	D	E	T	W	H	A	L	E

Page 10:

Birds have two legs.

Insects have six legs.

Spiders have eight legs.

Snakes don't have any legs.

Millipedes have so many legs it's hard to count!

Page 11:

Page 13: It's another spider!

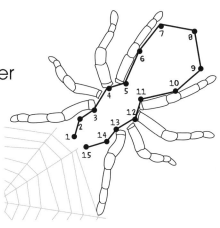

Page 14:

Page 15: You drew a dinosaur.

Page 17:

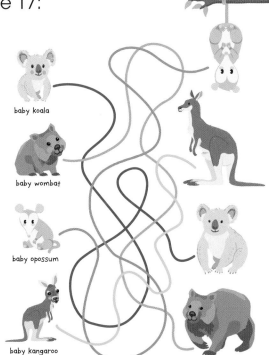

baby koala

baby wombat

baby opossum

baby kangaroo

Page 19:

Page 21: Footprint A is the goat, footprint B is the bear, footprint C is the horse

Page 23:

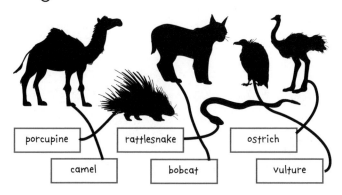

porcupine
camel
rattlesnake
bobcat
ostrich
vulture

Page 24:

Page 25: C, a fish does not spend time in trees.

Page 27:

Page 28:

E	T	H	G	M	A	N	D	H	P
J	E	A	R	T	H	W	O	R	M
C	S	E	O	T	I	R	R	R	F
A	G	A	U	C	E	R	M	S	J
N	O	C	N	G	E	P	O	T	X
T	O	A	D	A	A	L	U	I	E
A	I	A	H	M	V	N	S	B	E
C	B	R	O	G	O	N	E	B	H
B	L	C	G	L	L	I	G	A	S
S	F	O	X	T	E	H	E	R	E

Page 29:

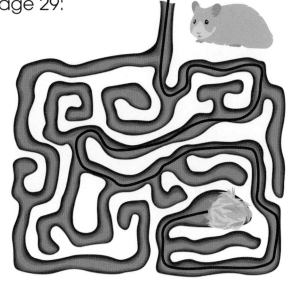

Page 31:

Page 35 top:

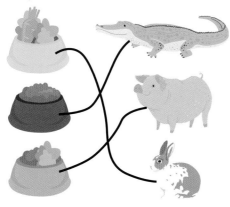

Page 35 bottom: 1) b, a herbivore.
2) false, they are carnivores

Page 37:

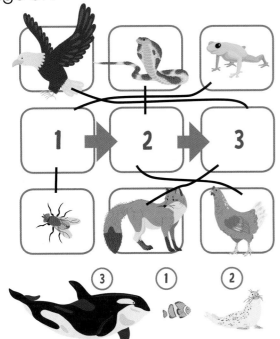

Page 39: a baby crocodile

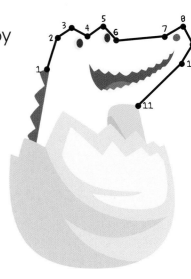

Page 40: 1) LAMB, 2) PIGLET 3) CALF 4) FOAL 5) KID 6) CHICK

Page 41: A) chick B) foal C) kid D) calf E) piglet F) lamb

Page 43:

Page 44: 1) b - nocturnal 2) a - insects have six legs 3) False - predators have eyes at the front of their face 4) a - elephants don't lay eggs 5) c - plants make their own food